Symphony No. 40
in G Minor, K550

&

Symphony No. 41
in C Major, K551
"Jupiter"

Wolfgang Amadeus
MOZART

DOVER PUBLICATIONS, INC.
Mineola, New York

Published in Canada by General Publishing Company, Ltd., 30 Lesmill Road, Don Mills, Toronto, Ontario.
Published in the United Kingdom by Constable and Company, Ltd., 3 The Lanchesters, 162–164 Fulham Palace Road, London W6 9ER.

Bibliographical Note

This Dover edition, first published in 1997, is a republication of Symphonies Nos. 40 and 41 in "Serie 8. Symphonien," Vol. 3, of *Wolfgang Amadeus Mozart's Werke, Kritisch durchgesehene Gesammtausgabe*, originally published by Breitkopf & Härtel, Leipzig, in 1880–1882.

International Standard Book Number: 0-486-29849-3

Manufactured in the United States of America
Dover Publications, Inc., 31 East 2nd Street, Mineola, N.Y. 11501

CONTENTS

Symphony No. 40
in G Minor, K550
(1788)

&

Symphony No. 41
in C Major, K551
(1788)

Symphony No. 40

INSTRUMENTATION

Flute [Flauto]
2 Oboes* [Oboi]
2 Clarinets* in B♭ ("B") [Clarinetti]
2 Bassoons [Fagotti]

2 Horns in E♭, G, B♭-alto
[Corni (Es, G, B-alto)]

Violins I, II [Violino]
Violas
Cellos & Basses
[Violoncello e Basso]

Symphony No. 41

INSTRUMENTATION

Flute [Flauto]
2 Oboes [Oboi]
2 Bassoons [Fagotti]

2 Horns in C, F [Corni]
2 Trumpets in C [Trombe]

Timpani

Violins I, II [Violino]
Violas
Cellos & Basses
[Violoncello e Basso]

*Mozart's woodwind scoring for Symphony No. 40 originally called for flute, two oboes and two bassoons. Clarinets were added in the composer's later revision. The present edition includes both versions: (a) the revised oboe/clarinet parts are printed at the top of each system; (b) the original oboe parts are printed in the fourth staff of each system.

SYMPHONY No. 40
in G Minor, K 550

Completed July 25, 1788 in Vienna.

19

30

Trio. 43

Allegro assai.

Oboi.

Clarinetti in B.

Flauto.

Oboi.

Fagotti.

Corno in B alto.

Corno in G.

Violino I.

Violino II.

Viola.

Violoncello
e Basso.

Menuetto da capo.

SYMPHONY No. 41
in C Major, K 551 ("Jupiter")

Completed August 10, 1788 in Vienna.

Bassi

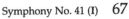

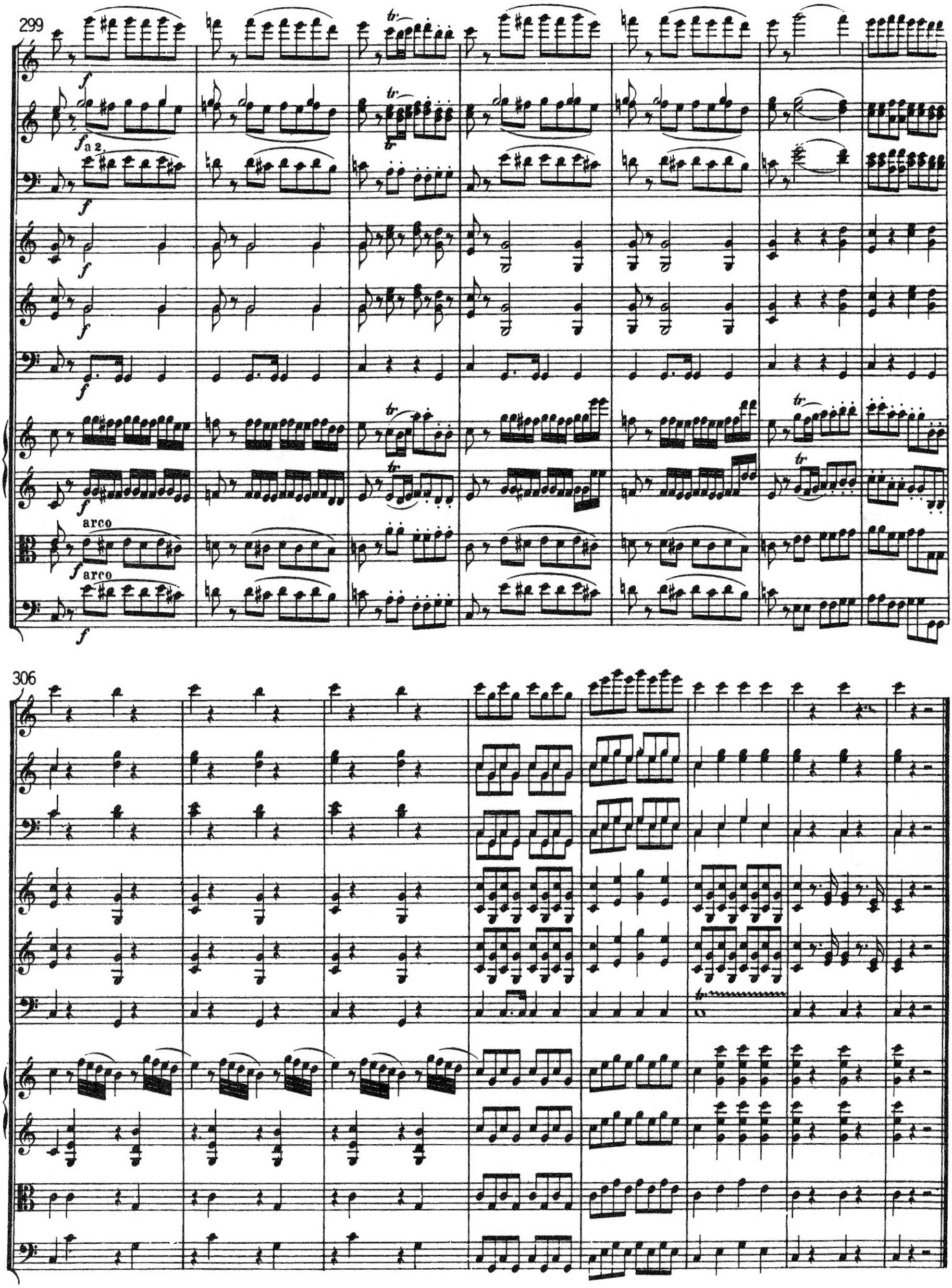
299
f
f a 2.
f
tr
f
f
arco
f
arco
f
306

70

Menuetto.

Menuetto da capo

85

END OF EDITION